Paris

You have kept photos and all sorts of mementoes
from your trips to Paris, and now you find yourself
with a unique collection, enough to awaken
your vocation to become a curator.
So as to avoid your favourite 'exhibits' getting hidden away in
an old shoe box, Elsa Editions is publishing this album
specially to give your souvenirs an ideal setting.

This interactive guide takes you back,
in text and pictures, to the atmosphere that gave
each itinerary its special charm.
You can then personalize it by including your own mementoes —
travel cards, museum tickets, restaurant menus, postcards,
bank notes etc. — in the pages designed for them.
You can include your own photos, so that the book becomes
a gentle wave of nostalgia, uniquely your own.

© 1998 Kingfisher Publications Plc
ISBN : 2-7452-0452-1

Memories

of

Paris

Along the Seine...

*Parisians have an unequalled love
for their river, and the millions of
visitors who come to Paris each year
agree with them.*

*The quays are an invitation to a
gentle, meditative stroll, or a long lovers' excursion.
The left and right banks reveal not only contrasts in the
grandiose architecture, but the very history of Paris itself.
For everyone, the Seine is a mirror of beauty and dreams.
The thirty or so bridges allow one to cross from one bank
to the other without breaking the spell.*

*The cathedral of Paris is the
outstanding monument in the Cité.
Since the XIVth century, it has
constituted a shining example
of both faith and gothic art, its
architecture reflecting its spiritual
universality. The interior of the immense cathedral has
a dazzling display of exuberant decoration in the 29
chapels of the transept and nave. The greatest artists
of the XVIIth century contributed to the splendour.
The statue of the Virgin and Child, known as Our Lady
of Paris, is an object of popular devotion as portrayed
in Victor Hugo's novel.*

Beaubourg, flagship of modern art

In the heart of the Halles, the Georges Pompidou Centre looks, according to its creators, like a spaceship or a giant mecano construction. It was devised to hold the National Museum of Modern Art, the Public Information Library (BPI) and the Institute for Acoustic and Musical Research (IRCAM).

The Beaubourg Centre has aroused many contradictory opinions, and is one of the shrines of modern creativity.

The museum's vast permanent collection includes works by Matisse, Picasso, Rothko, Kandinski, Braque, Chagall ...

The Place des Vosges, a royal square

Built on a swampy area of the right
bank, north of the Ile St Louis,
the Marais quarter is the site
of the Place des Vosges, a beautiful
square, and of some magnificent
Renaissance private residences.

Its streets and alleys are a constant
source of surprises for the stroller.
The Place des Vosges forms a square
with sides 140 metres

long, three of which contain shopping
arcades. The central garden, created under
Louis XIV for the use of the residents, was
a duelling ground, an activity forbidden
in the XVIIth century. In 1905, it was
converted into a park. The buildings round
it, with their admirably symmetrical
architecture, were home to the greatest
Parisian families.

Through the Marais ...

Since the XIVth century, the Marais has been prized by the Parisian nobility and upper classes.

Amid the austerity of stone and the exuberant decoration of private residences, the Marais retains a touch of the countryside. Here, in a shady courtyard, coolness, calm and discreet luxury give the Marais its unique character, a mixture of simplicity and aristocratic splendour — for benefit of its wealthy inhabitants ... and of strollers.

Between art and history

The Hôtel
de Sully was
built in 1624
and bought in
1634 by the Duke of Sully, faithful minister of Henri IV.
The vast inner courtyard presents harmonious façades
ornamented with sphinxes, scrolls and a series of low-
relief figures representing the Elements and the Seasons.
The Hôtel de Sully is still one of the most beautiful
private residences of the Marais, and is now the seat
of the National Office of Historical Monuments.
Temporary exhibitions take place there, and the lovely
garden gives access onto the Place des Vosges.

The Hôtel de Sens is one of the few
remaining private residences from
the Middle Ages. It is still in good
state, but the methods used for
its restoration have been hotly
contested. It was the residence
of Marguerite de Valois, 'Queen
Margot', the wife renounced
by Henri IV, who transformed it
into a palace of sensual pleasures.
Today it houses the Forney Library,
specializing in art and architecture.

To the Bastille...

On 14 July 1789, the seizure of the Bastille set off an attack on another institution, that of absolute monarchy. It was the starting point of the French Revolution. Later, in 1833, a bronze column was erected in the centre of the square in homage to the victims of the three days of revolution in July 1830, known as 'the Glorious Three'. To mark the bicentenary of the 1789 Revolution, the government had the glorious and ultra-sophisticated Bastille Opera House built, designed by Carlos Ott.

Today, the Bastille Opera House presents world-famous works of music. But it is far from the only cultural showplace in the quarter.

Paris with a difference ...

In this young, trendy and popular quarter, you can go from the port of the Arsenal in the south to St Martin's Canal in the north, and discover a very different atmosphere. To explore an unusual aspect of the Bastille quarter, you just have to go into the little courtyards and alleyways that are hidden behind the façades of the rue

du Faubourg St Antoine. Many artists have come to live here. The traditional cafés that are part of the charm of Paris are full of life again, particularly in the evenings ...

The Latin Quarter, intellect and liberty

The Latin Quarter has been and still is home to intellectuals and students. Since it was created in the XIIIth century, the Sorbonne University has been a major centre of learning, sited in the midst of some of the top lycées.

At the end of the boulevard St Michel, near the Seine, the fountain of St Michel is a popular meeting place for young people. Created by Davioud in 1860, it has a bronze statue of St Michael killing the dragon in the central recess. Luckily the two dragons that decorate the fountain only spout water ... often leading to refreshing water sports in the hot summer days or the quarter's lively nights.

The Pantheon, temple of fame

To the east of the wide
boulevard St Michel, the
Pantheon crowns the Mount
St Genevieve. Soufflot was the
moving force behind this building, which was constructed
on the site of the old St Genevieve Abbey church, but
he died ten years before work was finished. Completed
in 1790, the church was transformed into a burial place
for the illustrious dead of France.
You can go and wander round
the Luxembourg Gardens by passing
through the peaceful gardens
of the Observatory. Also known as
'the Luco', the Luxembourg Gardens
boast many fine statues and the
Medici Fountain. Queen Marie
dei Medici bought the land from
the Carthusians in 1615, and had
the splendid Florentine palace built.
Since 1958 it has been the seat
of the Senate.

The cafe terraces of St Germain

When you think of St Germain des Prés, the names of the people who made the quarter famous in the postwar years inevitably come to mind: Boris Vian, Juliette Gréco, Jean-Paul Sartre and Simone de Beauvoir ... but it is also the cafés, jazz cellars, book shops and art galleries that gave St Germain its 'trendily intellectual' reputation.

In the Place St Germain, you get the best view of the church, and of passers-by, from the terrace of the Deux Magots café, surrounded by the laughter and chat from the other tables. Like the Deux Magots, the Café Flore is famous as one of the favourite meeting-places of intellectuals.

The left bank quays

On the Conti and Malaquais quays, you will find the School of Fine Arts, the Institute of France (which is home to the French Academy) and the Mint. Symbols of art, knowledge and wealth, these 'great houses of France' are a source of national pride, and also bring prestige to these banks of the Seine where once Voltaire and Baudelaire, among others, lived.

Near the Seine on the Malaquais quay, the prestigious Paris School of Fine Arts, founded in 1816, occupies the remains of the old convent of the Petits Augustins (XVIIth century), the Hôtel de Chimay (XVIIIth century) and some XIXth century buildings, notably the Loges (exam rooms) constructed by Duret around 1820.

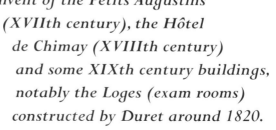

Visiting the Orsay Museum

Orsay Station, constructed by Victor Laloux for the Universal Exhibition in 1900, is now one of the most beautiful museums in Paris, and attracts crowds of visitors from all over the world. The museum holds some splendid collections, mostly coming from the Louvre and the Jeu de Paume Museum, in particular Impressionist masterpieces.

Inaugurated in December 1986, the Orsay Museum has managed to respect and preserve the original structure

and character of the former station in which it is sited. This fine example of cast-iron and glass architecture, which shows to advantage the great nave of the central aisle, does full justice to the works of art it now holds. On the façade that borders the quays, statues representing Bordeaux, Toulouse and Nantes are reminders of the destinations formerly served by the station.

The Invalides, witness to past glories

Behind its long classical façade, the fine Hôtel des
Invalides has 17 courtyards and covers ten hectares.
Founded by Louis XIV to house his wounded soldiers,
his monument was, according to him 'the most
important idea of his reign'.

The Hôtel des Invalides is the masterpiece of Libéral
Bruant, who worked on it from 1671 to 1676.
The dome of the chapel was designed
by Hardouin-Mansart in 1679 and
completed in 1706. Regilded in 1989
with 12 kilos of gold, it holds
the tomb of Napoleon I, guarded by
numerous captured enemy cannons.

The 'Great Lady' of Paris

Dominating the Champs de Mars park, 320 metres above the Seine, the Eiffel Tower looks out over Paris. This imperturbable sentinel with its head in the clouds is illuminated at night, showing off to advantage the intricate lace of its ironwork. While marking the triumph of technical progress and metal architecture, the great engineer Gustave Eiffel also contrived to give this gigantic skeleton an aesthetic element.

The most beautiful avenue in the world …

*Whether you go
up or down the
Champs Elysées, you travel
along the most beautiful
avenue in the world. Formerly
a fashionable promenade,
today this great highway is an immense and lively
thoroughfare, and the lights of its shop window displays
are the stuff of dreams.*

*The Champs Elysées are home to the most prestigious
addresses in Paris: not only is it the site of the greatest
names in haute couture
and luxury goods, it is also
the quarter of top hotels
and the presidential
palace.*

With your back to the Arc de Triomphe, you find that
the most beautiful avenue in the world opens onto …
the most beautiful square in the world,
Concorde. A junction of breathtaking perspectives, the
Place de la Concorde opens onto the Champs Elysées,
the Madeleine, the Tuileries Gardens and, across the

Seine, the National Assembly.
This makes it one of the most
beautiful crossroads in Paris.
A present from the Pasha
Mehemet Ali to Louis Philippe
in 1831 and erected in 1836,
the Luxor Obelisk, covered
with heiroglyphics, recounts
the exploits of the Pharoah
Ramses II. This imposing
monolith marks the centre
of the square, designed by
Jacques-Anges Gabriel
and inaugurated in 1763.

The Louvre, a palace of kings, a museum for the world

*The Louvre Palace was the
residence of the kings of France
for nearly four centuries.
It was François I who, in
the XVIth century, having built
a Renaissance palace on the site, donated its first works
of art. It was this sovereign, with
a passion for Italian art, who acquired
the celebrated painting by Leonardo
da Vinci, the Mona Lisa, whose mysterious
smile continues
to fascinate visitors
to the museum.*

The Opera, a shrine to dance

This quarter
is centred
around the
Opera, designed by
Charles Garnier, and now
mainly devoted to dance.

Started in 1862, it was inaugurated in
1875. This building, a symbol of the Second
Empire, is a mixture of just about all
known styles, from classical to baroque,
and finally the ultimate example
of the style of Napoleon III.

In the interior is a magnificent staircase, its volutes
leading the way to the auditorium with its ceiling
painted by Chagall.

On the Butte Montmartre, around Sacré Cœur

In the heart of the Butte, the place du Tertre is full of colour. Tourists and locals mix to form a motley crowd. In this former 'Free Commune of Montmartre', founded in 1871 against the Versailles authorities, you can allow yourself a pause on a café terrace to listen to Aristide Bruant's traditional songs, accompanied by an accordion.

A walk around the Butte is like a stroll in a steep-sloped village, down twisting streets full of memories of famous artists and writers: Toulouse Lautrec, Renoir, Van Gogh, Gauguin, Cézanne, Utrillo, Valadon, Modigliani, Braque, Apollinaire, Picasso …

Versailles, the Sun King's palace

In the XVIIth century, the Louvre
palace, already a royal residence,
became too small to contain
the ambitions of King Louis XIV
and his court, which
was numerous and demanding.
The Sun King therefore decided to install
himself in Versailles, outside Paris,
and to have a grandiose palace built
there, to reflect his power and his glory.
He hoped too to be able to devote himself
to his passion for hunting there, and
to keep his dissenting nobles more
securely under his eye.

From 1668, Hardouin-Mansart and Le Vau
directed the enormous construction
site, which was to become the most
beautiful palace in the world. It
is true that the Sun King's
megalomania was equalled
only by his desire to please,
seduce and impress the most
humble of his subjects as much
as his noble guests.

Luxury, power and beauty ...

The painter Charles Le Brun devoted all his art and talent to the king's service, solely to ensure that the harmonization and interior decoration reflected the magnificence that Louis XIV demanded.

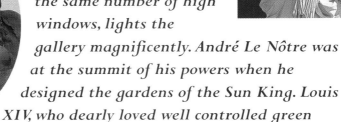

The 17 huge mirrors of the Hall of Mirrors, facing the same number of high windows, lights the gallery magnificently. André Le Nôtre was at the summit of his powers when he designed the gardens of the Sun King. Louis XIV, who dearly loved well controlled green spaces, sought to organize the universe as he did his gardens. The Versailles park was laid out before the palace, and inspired the king to write a book titled How Best to Show Off the Versailles Gardens. Alleys, fountains and statues are its outstanding features.

Impressions

of
Paris

Impression Grafica Editoriale - Bologne
Dépôt légal : Octobre 1998
(Printed in Italy)